PRAYERSCRIPTS

PARDON
THROUGH THE
BLOOD

60 DAYS OF
PRAYERS FOR
TOTAL
FORGIVENESS
& FREEDOM

CYRIL OPOKU

Published by *Quest Publications*

ISBN: 978-1-988439-68-6

Cover design by *Quest Publications (questpublications@outlook.com)*

Unless otherwise indicated, all Scripture quotations are taken from the World English Bible WEB, which is in the public domain. For more information, visit: www.worldenglish.bible

This book is a work of devotional encouragement. It is not intended to replace biblical study, pastoral counsel, or professional therapy.

Printed in the United States of America.

First Edition: July 2025

For more books like this, visit *PrayerScripts:* https://prayerscripts.org

CONTENTS

PREFACE

"In whom we have our redemption through his blood, the forgiveness of our trespasses, according to the riches of his grace."
— *Ephesians 1:14 WEB*

T here is no greater gift than forgiveness. At the heart of the gospel is this radiant truth: we are not merely improved— we are redeemed, cleansed, and forgiven by the blood of Jesus Christ. This book was birthed out of a deep conviction that many believers live beneath their spiritual inheritance, weighed down by guilt, cycles of sin, and a distorted view of God's mercy. *Pardon Through the Blood* was written to break that cycle.

Every prayer and Scripture in this book is soaked in the revelation of the blood covenant. This is not just about knowing we're forgiven—it's about living forgiven. It's about boldly embracing the full pardon Jesus paid for with His life, walking free from condemnation, and standing in the righteousness He alone provides. These prayers are crafted not for casual recitation but for Spirit-filled declaration. They are for the weary soul, the repentant heart, the intercessor crying out for their family, and the believer ready to claim the finished work of Christ.

As you pray through these pages, may chains break, shame lift, and a new awareness of God's mercy flood your life. Let this journey renew your confidence in the cross, deepen your intimacy with the Father, and awaken your faith in the power of the blood.

We have been pardoned—fully, eternally, and irrevocably—through the blood. Let us walk in it.

For the glory of His grace,

Cyril O.

Illinois, July 2025

INTRODUCTION

There is a voice louder than shame. A power stronger than guilt. A cleansing deeper than the darkest stain of sin. That voice is the blood of Jesus, and it still speaks today.

P*ardon Through the Blood* invites you into a holy encounter with the Lamb of God, who takes away the sins of the world—not by overlooking them, but by paying for them in full. Every drop of Christ's blood poured out on Calvary was a divine proclamation: **You are forgiven. You are free. You are loved.**

This book is not a theology manual—it is a *prayer companion*. You will journey through 60 blood-specific Scriptures, each one paired with a prophetic, Spirit-filled prayer designed to lead you and your family into the full reality of divine pardon. Whether you carry the weight of past failures, wrestle with cycles of condemnation, or simply hunger for deeper intimacy with the Father, these pages will guide you into the cleansing stream of Christ's sacrifice.

Each prayer is rooted in Scripture, spoken in faith, and infused with heaven's authority. As you declare them over your life, your household, and your lineage, may you experience the supernatural freedom that only the blood of Jesus can secure.

Come boldly. Come broken. Come believing.

You have been pardoned—now walk in it.

How to Use This Book

This book is designed to be more than just read—it's meant to be prayed, spoken, and lived.

Each day, you'll encounter a blood-related Scripture, a themed prayer focus, and a prophetic prayer declaration. These prayers are intentionally crafted to help you and your family receive and walk in the full pardon Christ purchased through His blood. The goal is not religious routine, but *spiritual renewal*.

Here's how to make the most of each entry:

1. **Read the Scripture Slowly and Out Loud.** Let it settle into your heart. Speak it with reverence, knowing it carries the power of God's voice and covenant promise.

2. **Reflect on the Themed Focus.** Whether it's cleansing, forgiveness, or freedom from accusation, pause to consider how this truth applies to your current season.

3. **Pray the Prophetic Prayer Boldly.** Don't just skim it—*own* it. Pray as one standing under the blood of Jesus. Declare the words over yourself, your family, your children, and your legacy. You are waging war against shame, guilt, and spiritual bondage.

4. **Journal or Activate.** Consider journaling what God speaks to you through each prayer or take a simple action step: forgive someone, repent, take communion, or speak words of blessing over your household.

5. **Repeat as Needed.** These prayers are not one-time events. Let them become part of your spiritual arsenal. Return to them when condemnation whispers, when the past resurfaces, or when a loved one needs divine mercy.

You can use this book over 60 days, revisit specific themes weekly, or allow the Spirit to lead you day by day. However you move through it, do so with faith—believing that the blood still speaks.

Welcome to the covenant of pardon. Your redemption is not partial. It is complete.

DAY 1

Redeemed by the Blood of Jesus

"In him we have our redemption through his blood, the forgiveness of our trespasses, according to the riches of his grace."
— Ephesians 1:7 WEB

O Redeemer of my soul, I boldly stand in the assurance that I have been purchased and pardoned by the blood of Jesus. I do not come by works or by merit, but by the riches of grace that have been poured out for me and my household. I declare that Your mercy has triumphed over judgment, and Your forgiveness has silenced every accusation. Through the blood, I have been brought near—cleansed, accepted, and beloved.

Father, I apply this redemption to every failure, secret struggle, and generational stain that has plagued my life or family line. Let the blood that speaks better things than judgment echo through the foundations of our history, and silence every voice of condemnation. Let cycles of guilt and shame break now under the weight of divine mercy. I declare that my lineage is free—my children and descendants walk in holy liberty.

Because of the blood, I decree that no stain remains. We are redeemed from bondage, delivered from darkness, and restored to our rightful inheritance in You. The blood has spoken, and the verdict is final: we are forgiven, cleansed, and forever Yours.

In Jesus' name, Amen.

DAY 2

Justified From All Wrath

"Much more then, being now justified by his blood, we
will be saved from God's wrath through him."
— Romans 5:9 WEB

Righteous Judge and Merciful Savior, I stand today not in fear but
in boldness, because I have been justified by the precious blood of
Jesus. The wrath that was due me and my family has been turned
away—not by pleading, but by the poured-out sacrifice of the
Lamb. The blood has settled every legal case brought against me in
the courts of Heaven, and I am declared righteous in Your sight.

I lift my voice and declare over my family: no wrath, no curse, no
judgment shall overtake us, for the blood has covered us fully. The
accusations of the enemy hold no power; the shame of past sins no
longer sticks to our name. Because of this divine justification, peace
is our portion and reconciliation is our inheritance. The blood
speaks innocence over our household.

We shall not live under torment or spiritual backlash, but walk in
the confidence of those who are covered, justified, and secured by
Christ. The blood is our refuge, and its voice shields us from every
storm of divine wrath or human attack. We live in the shelter of
mercy.

In Jesus' name, Amen.

DAY 3

Cleansed and Walking in Light

"But if we walk in the light as he is in the light, we have
fellowship with one another, and the blood of Jesus Christ,
his Son, cleanses us from all sin."
— 1 John 1:7 WEB

Light of the World, I come into the brilliance of Your presence, leaving every hidden place behind. I declare that my life and my family are aligned with truth, transparency, and the purifying fellowship of Your Spirit. Because of the blood of Jesus, we are not stained by sin, but daily washed and renewed.

Father, I receive the continual cleansing that flows from the cross—cleansing of thoughts, words, and actions. Let the blood purify our conscience, reset our desires, and bring us into a holy rhythm of righteousness. I break every power of habitual sin and secret darkness; let Your blood flood the deepest recesses of our hearts and drive out all impurity.

Because of the blood, we walk in unity—no strife, no bitterness, no walls of division. Let Your peace govern our relationships. Let fellowship flourish where there was once isolation. Our home shall be a sanctuary of light, love, and truth, all held together by the cleansing power of the blood.

In Jesus' name, Amen.

DAY 4

Freed from Shame and Filth

"To him who loves us and washed us from our sins by his
blood..."
— Revelation 1:5 WEB

O Faithful and True, how marvelous is Your love, that You would
reach into the depths of my guilt and wash me clean. I declare that
Your blood has not just covered my sins but has removed them,
washed them away like stains from a garment. I am not who I
was—my identity is no longer tethered to my failures.

By the authority of Your blood, I break the hold of shame, regret,
and condemnation over myself and my family. Every memory that
accuses, every whisper of the past that seeks to haunt—be silenced
now by the blood. I decree emotional healing over our minds,
restoration over our names, and dignity over our destiny.

We are loved, washed, and welcomed. Because of the blood, I lift
my head high and lead my household in the assurance that we are
clean, consecrated, and called. What once defiled us no longer
defines us. We have been made new, and nothing shall separate us
from Your love.

In Jesus' name, Amen.

DAY 5

PURGED FOR PURE SERVICE

"How much more will the blood of Christ... cleanse your conscience from dead works to serve the living God?"
— Hebrews 9:14 WEB

O Living God, I thank You for the blood of Your Son that not only forgives but transforms. I stand today, fully aware that Your blood has gone beyond surface cleansing—it has reached the core of my conscience. I am no longer bound to perform or strive for Your approval; the blood has freed me to serve You in spirit and in truth.

I renounce every dead work, every empty ritual, every legalistic attempt to earn Your favor. By the blood, I am delivered from guilt-driven religion and brought into peace-filled relationship. Let my heart beat in rhythm with grace. Let my family serve not out of fear but from love ignited by redemption.

Because of the blood, our service shall be joyful, Spirit-empowered, and fruitful. We are cleansed for purpose, purified for assignment, and prepared for glory. I decree a household of servants who live to make Your name known, unburdened by the weight of yesterday.

In Jesus' name, Amen.

DAY 6

RESCUED FROM DARKNESS INTO LIGHT

"In whom we have our redemption, the forgiveness of our sins."
— Colossians 1:14 WEB

Rescuing King, I exalt You for the blood that tore me from the grip of darkness and brought me into the light of forgiveness. I was once imprisoned by guilt and shame, but now I live in liberty. My family and I have been transferred—we no longer live under the domain of the enemy.

The blood of Jesus has paid our ransom. I speak it over every pattern of failure, every generational grip of sin, every spiritual stronghold: you have no hold. We are forgiven, and forgiveness is our banner. I declare that no darkness shall prevail over this household, because the blood has marked our doorway.

Let Your light invade our minds, our emotions, our children's destinies. I speak breakthrough where there's been bondage, clarity where confusion reigned, and holiness where impurity once ruled. We walk in redemption power, fearless and forgiven.

In Jesus' name, Amen.

DAY 7

Boldness to Enter God's Presence

"Having therefore, brothers, boldness to enter into the
holy place by the blood of Jesus..."
— Hebrews 10:19 WEB

Holy God, because of the blood of Jesus, I come boldly—not
timidly—into Your presence. I do not shrink back, for the veil has
been torn, and the invitation extended. The blood has granted
access to You, and I bring my family into this holy place with me.

I apply this blood-bought boldness to every prayer I utter, every
request I make, and every mountain I face. Let fear and inferiority
be silenced now. Let my children know the nearness of Your glory.
Let our home be a dwelling place of divine communion, where
intimacy with You is not occasional but continual.

No more distance, no more striving. The blood has qualified us. I
declare that my family lives under an open heaven, and our prayers
rise with confidence, reaching the very heart of God. We are not
castaways—we are covenant children.

In Jesus' name, Amen.

DAY 8

COVENANT OF FORGIVENESS SEALED

"For this is my blood of the new covenant, which is poured out for many for the remission of sins."
— Matthew 26:28 WEB

Covenant-Keeping God, I honor the precious blood of Jesus, poured out not in part but in full for my sins. This is no ordinary promise—this is the eternal agreement signed in blood, guaranteeing that I am forever forgiven. No power in hell can revoke what You have sealed.

I apply this covenant over my family. Every iniquity is blotted out, every transgression erased, every hidden fault cleansed. Let generational burdens be broken by this blood. I speak mercy into my bloodline, forgiveness into our story, and healing into our soul. The curse is canceled. The debt is paid.

We are not bound to our past—we are bound to You. And this covenant will never be broken. I rejoice that Your blood has done what no man could do: secure my standing and guarantee my freedom.

In Jesus' name, Amen.

DAY 9

LIFE-GIVING BLOOD FOR MY FAMILY

"For the life of the flesh is in the blood..."
— Leviticus 17:11 WEB

Breath of Life, I give thanks for the living blood of Jesus, which has become the source of eternal life for me and my family. I declare that this blood is not symbolic—it is supernatural. It carries divine life into every fiber of my being.

I speak life over every dying place, every weary soul, every weakened body. Where depression once ruled, let the blood speak joy. Where fear once gripped, let courage arise. Where sickness lurked, let resurrection power flood in. Your blood is our life source—constant, eternal, and unstoppable.

Let our children live and not die. Let our legacy be marked by vitality, fruitfulness, and flourishing in spirit and soul. I cover my home with this living blood and declare: life flows here, and death has no dominion.

In Jesus' name, Amen.

DAY 10

WITHOUT BLOOD, NO FORGIVENESS

"Without shedding of blood there is no remission."
— Hebrews 9:22 WEB

Most Holy God, I acknowledge the unshakable truth: there is no forgiveness without the blood. Not one of my sins was excused—they were paid for. I worship You for the blood of Jesus, which did not overlook my sin but washed it away.

Let this truth saturate my soul and silence every lie of unworthiness. I do not earn Your mercy—I receive it, because the blood has been shed. Over my family I proclaim: no condemnation remains, no sin is left uncovered. The blood has made full remission. Our record is clean, and our hearts are free.

Thank You for the justice and mercy that met at the cross. I will never treat the blood lightly. It is my banner, my defense, my covering, and my peace.

In Jesus' name, Amen.

DAY 11

WASHED WHITER THAN SNOW

"Though your sins be as scarlet, they shall be as white as snow."
— Isaiah 1:18 WEB

Merciful Father, I run into the arms of grace today, overwhelmed by the power of Your mercy and the cleansing blood of Jesus. Where my sin had stained me crimson, You have made me white as snow. I stand in awe that nothing in my past—no action, thought, or word—has been too dark for Your redemption. The blood has blotted out every stain and restored me to innocence.

Let this supernatural cleansing flow over my family. I bring before You the failures of generations, the hidden faults, and the repeated patterns that have bound us. Wash us, Lord—not only from what we've done but from what we've become. Purify our memories, our emotions, our identities. Let guilt fall off like chains. Let purity rise up like dawn.

I declare over my household: we are not marked by shame, but by grace. Not scarlet, but snow-white. Not stained, but sanctified. Let our lives testify to the transforming power of mercy. Because of the blood, we are made clean and made new.

In Jesus' name, Amen.

DAY 12

THE LAMB WHO BORE IT ALL

"Behold, the Lamb of God, who takes away the sin of the
world!"
— John 1:29 WEB

Jesus, Lamb of God, I behold You today with fresh wonder and
profound gratitude. You carried my sins—all of them—not in part,
but in whole. You bore the weight of my failures, the shame of my
rebellion, and the wrath that should have been mine. Thank You for
taking it all upon Yourself and setting me free.

I lift up my voice in thanksgiving for Your selfless love. You did not
look away from my mess. You stepped into it, wrapped Yourself in
humanity, and became my Substitute. For me, and for my family,
You became the Lamb—the perfect sacrifice who ended the reign
of sin with one final offering. No more striving. No more
punishment. No more debt.

Today, I exalt You as our sin-bearer. May my home be filled with
songs of gratitude and reverence for the Lamb. May we live in the
freedom You've purchased and never take lightly the blood that was
shed. Because You took away our sin, we will live in joy, liberty, and
righteousness all our days.

In Jesus' name, Amen.

DAY 13

The Blood On Our Doorposts

"When I see the blood, I will pass over you."
— Exodus 12:13 WEB

O Covenant-Keeping God, I plead the blood of Jesus over my life, over my household, over every doorway of our lives. Just as the Israelites marked their homes with lamb's blood for protection, I mark our family with the eternal blood of the Lamb of God. Let every judgment pass over us. Let every plague turn away.

Father, I decree divine exemption from destruction. We are not exposed to the wrath that sweeps the earth—we are covered. Let no disease, disaster, or demonic attack breach the boundary of Your covenant. The blood is our defense, our shield, our banner. It cries out "Mercy!" over our home, and You see it and honor it.

I declare that fear will not rule us, because the blood speaks louder than the threat. We are hidden under the shadow of the Almighty, covered in covenant and wrapped in redemption. Let angels encamp around us. Let peace dwell within our walls. Because of the blood, we are safe, spared, and sealed.

In Jesus' name, Amen.

DAY 14

Healed Through His Wounds

"He was wounded for our transgressions..."
— Isaiah 53:5 WEB

Suffering Servant, I honor You for the stripes You bore and the wounds You endured for me and my family. You were crushed for what we did wrong—wounded so we could be healed, chastised so we could have peace. Every lash, every bruise, every drop of blood shouted love louder than our sin ever could.

Today, I apply the healing virtue of Your blood to our lives. Let healing flow into every sickness, every trauma, every place of brokenness. From the crown of our heads to the soles of our feet, let Your stripes bring restoration. Emotionally, mentally, physically—we receive the full benefit of Your suffering.

We will not live under the dominion of pain or shame. Because You were wounded, we are whole. Because You bled, we are healed. I declare over my family that sickness must bow, torment must flee, and peace must reign. We are the healed of the Lord—set free by the power of the Cross.

In Jesus' name, Amen.

DAY 15

FAITH IN THE BLOOD ALONE

"Whom God sent to be an atoning sacrifice, through faith
in his blood…"
— Romans 3:25 WEB

Righteous Judge and Gracious Redeemer, my faith today is not in
my own goodness but in the blood of Jesus. You presented Him as
the atoning sacrifice—not hidden, but publicly displayed—so that
I could place my trust in His blood alone. That blood justifies me,
covers me, and grants me peace with You.

Let faith rise in my spirit and saturate my household. Let my
children, my spouse, and generations after me walk in bold trust,
not in works but in the power of the blood. I reject guilt and
religion, and I embrace the finished work of Christ. The blood has
settled the case, and I believe it fully.

I decree that we will not waver in our standing. Our righteousness
is not fragile—it is founded on blood that speaks forever. We have
access, acceptance, and assurance through faith. Let our lives reflect
the confidence of those who trust in the blood of the Lamb.

In Jesus' name, Amen.

DAY 16

Precious Blood, Priceless Ransom

"Redeemed… with precious blood, as of a lamb without
blemish…"
— 1 Peter 1:18–19 WEB

Holy and Worthy Lord, I lift my heart in reverence for the precious
blood that redeemed me—not with silver or gold, but with the
priceless blood of Jesus, the spotless Lamb. I was ransomed from an
empty, cursed way of living and brought into the richness of divine
inheritance.

Lord, help me never treat this blood as common. Let awe flood my
soul every time I think of what it cost You to redeem me. Over my
family, I release the revelation of value and worth. We are not cheap.
We are not forgotten. We were purchased with the highest price
ever paid.

Let this truth establish our identity and silence every lie of
worthlessness or rejection. I declare that the precious blood of Jesus
has made us royalty, and we will live as sons and daughters of the
King. Because of the blood, we are redeemed, restored, and revered
in Your eyes.

In Jesus' name, Amen.

DAY 17

SET APART BY HIS BLOOD

"That he might sanctify the people through his own blood..."
— Hebrews 13:12 WEB

Sanctifying Savior, I praise You for the blood that not only saves but separates. You did not just redeem me to rescue me—you redeemed me to set me apart for Yourself. The blood has marked my life, and I will never be the same. I belong to You, and my household belongs to You.

Let this sanctifying power touch every area of my life. Purge our minds from compromise, our habits from corruption, our homes from every unclean thing. Set a boundary of holiness around my family, that we may live consecrated lives in a generation of confusion. The blood has drawn the line—we are set apart.

Let our actions reflect this calling. Let our words, decisions, and relationships be drenched in purity. May Your name be honored in our home. The blood has sanctified us, and we receive the grace to walk worthy of the calling we've received.

In Jesus' name, Amen.

DAY 18

COMPLETELY WASHED AND RESTORED

"You were washed, you were sanctified, you were justified…"
— 1 Corinthians 6:11 WEB

Cleansing Fountain, I rejoice in the finished work of redemption. I am not what I used to be. I have been washed clean by Your blood, sanctified by Your Spirit, and justified in Your sight. Every accusation has been overturned, every stain removed. I walk in complete restoration.

Thank You, Lord, for the totality of what You've done. This is no halfway salvation—it's full and final. My family is not partly clean—we are fully restored. Let every generational shame fall away. Let every voice of the enemy be silenced. The blood declares us clean.

We will live like those who are free—no longer chained by sin, but empowered by grace. We are washed vessels, holy instruments, and justified sons and daughters. Let this be the song of our lives: "We are clean. We are changed. We are Yours."

In Jesus' name, Amen.

DAY 19

ROBES WASHED IN THE BLOOD

"They washed their robes and made them white in the
Lamb's blood."
— Revelation 7:14 WEB

Lamb of God, I thank You for the blood that purifies like nothing
else. The saints in glory are clothed in radiant white—not because
of what they did, but because they washed their robes in Your
blood. So I come, Lord, and wash again. I bring my heart, my soul,
my household—we soak our garments in Your cleansing flow.

Let every spot be removed. Let every residue of compromise be
scrubbed away. I decree that we shall wear garments of praise, not
shame—robes of righteousness, not regret. I declare over my family
that we will not walk stained or disqualified. We are clothed in what
heaven calls holy.

Purity is our inheritance. Righteousness is our portion. Because of
the blood, we are prepared for Your presence, dressed for glory, and
ready for eternal purpose. Let the world see the evidence of the
blood in how we walk, speak, and shine.

In Jesus' name, Amen.

DAY 20

FORGIVEN AND FOREVER FREE

"As far as the east is from the west, so far has he removed our transgressions from us."
— Psalm 103:12 WEB

Faithful Father, I praise You for the blood that has not just forgiven, but completely removed my sins. You didn't sweep them under the rug or keep a record to remind me later. You've cast them far away—so far that they will never return. This is the power of redemption.

I declare that my family will no longer live under the shadow of past mistakes. What was done has been undone by the cross. What was broken has been restored. Let the blood remove every guilt-laced memory, every generational iniquity, every trace of condemnation. We are free—truly free.

Let this freedom bring joy to our household. Let laughter return. Let peace dwell here. We are not bound by what was—we are driven by who You've made us to be. As far as the east is from the west, so far have You removed it all. Hallelujah!

In Jesus' name, Amen.

DAY 21

SINS CAST INTO THE SEA

"You will cast all their sins into the depths of the sea."
— Micah 7:19 WEB

Gracious Redeemer, I thank You for Your incomprehensible mercy. You do not deal with us according to our sins, nor remember them forever. You don't just forgive; You cast them into the deepest sea, never to be retrieved. What You have removed cannot return. I rest in the assurance that the blood of Jesus has caused You to forget what once separated me from You.

Lord, I lift up every lingering sense of guilt in my heart and home. Let Your mercy wash over my family. Where we have replayed mistakes and carried shame like baggage, help us release it fully into the ocean of Your forgiveness. Let this truth saturate our hearts: when You forgive, You forget. We don't need to perform, strive, or rehearse our failures again.

Let the memory of sin be replaced with the memory of grace. May we live boldly as those completely pardoned, not because we deserved it, but because Jesus paid for it in full. Our sins are not hidden—they're gone. Buried. Sunk forever in mercy's sea.

In Jesus' name, Amen.

DAY 22

Blotted Out and Made New

"Repent… so that your sins may be blotted out…"
— Acts 3:19 WEB

Father of Compassion, I come with a heart willing to turn. You call me not just to confess but to repent, to turn from sin and step into newness. And when I do, You blot out my sins—not smudge, not edit—You erase them completely. Thank You for such restoration and the invitation to return to You wholeheartedly.

Let the grace of repentance flood my household. May we not see it as punishment but as a door back to joy. Let our hearts be quick to yield, quick to respond, and quick to return. Where hardness has crept in, soften us. Where cycles of sin remain, break them with holy sorrow that leads to life.

I declare that times of refreshing are coming. Our sins are being blotted out—removed from the record, washed from our conscience, and replaced with righteousness. We are not defined by what we've done, but by the mercy that met us when we turned. We choose the path of repentance that leads to restoration.

In Jesus' name, Amen.

DAY 23

No More Condemnation

"There is therefore now no condemnation…"
— Romans 8:1 WEB

Lord Jesus, thank You for breaking the voice of condemnation in my life. Because of Your blood, I no longer live under the weight of judgment or guilt. I am not condemned—I am forgiven, accepted, and free. You have declared me not guilty, and Your word is final.

I silence every voice that says otherwise. Whether it's my past, my feelings, or the enemy himself, they no longer get to define me. There is now—right now—no condemnation. The blood has made peace between me and God. Let this truth saturate my soul and renew my mind.

Over my family, I declare freedom from shame. No more hiding. No more beating ourselves up. We will live as children of the light, bold and secure. The cross settled it, and the blood speaks mercy, not accusation. We are covered, clean, and confident.

In Jesus' name, Amen.

DAY 24

RIGHTEOUS BY HIS BLOOD

For him who knew no sin he made to be sin on our behalf;
so that in him we might become the righteousness of God.
—2 Corinthians 5:21 WEB

Holy God, how can it be that You would make me righteous? Jesus, You took on my sin, my shame, and my punishment so that I could be made right with God. This is not a borrowed righteousness—it's a divine exchange. You wore my sin so I could wear Your purity.

Help me walk in this reality every day. Let me stop striving for approval and start standing in the identity You've given. I am the righteousness of God—not because of my performance, but because of the blood that covers me. Let that truth shape how I think, speak, and live.

Over my family, I release this identity. We are not bound by guilt or defined by past failures. We are clothed in righteousness, royal in standing, and beloved in Your eyes. Let the boldness of that truth propel us into purpose.

In Jesus' name, Amen.

DAY 25

WASHED AND RENEWED

"...he saved us... by the washing of regeneration..."
— Titus 3:5 WEB

Father of Renewal, I thank You for the spiritual washing that made me new. It wasn't by works or religion, but by Your mercy. You poured out Your Spirit and washed away everything old. You gave me new birth, new identity, and a new heart. The blood of Jesus didn't just forgive me—it transformed me.

Let this renewing flow over every part of me. Cleanse my thoughts, purify my desires, and restore what sin has damaged. Let Your Spirit regenerate areas I thought were beyond hope. Over my family, bring renewal—revive what's been weary, refresh what's been dry, and make all things new.

I declare we are not who we used to be. The old has passed, the new has come. We've been washed in mercy's fountain, and we are being daily renewed by Your Spirit. Let that freshness mark our home, our faith, and our walk with You.

In Jesus' name, Amen.

DAY 26

LIVING BY FAITH IN THE BLOOD

"I live… by faith in the Son of God, who loved me and gave himself for me."
— Galatians 2:20 WEB

Jesus, I thank You for the life I now live—it's not mine alone, but Yours living through me. You loved me and gave Yourself for me, and because of that, I no longer live by sight or effort but by faith in Your blood. This is a daily walk of dependence and trust.

Let faith rise in me afresh today. Let it not be faith in circumstances, emotions, or my own strength, but faith in the unshakable sacrifice of Jesus. Your blood didn't just save me—it sustains me. Let that faith fuel my prayers, my decisions, and my vision.

Over my family, I release grace to live by this same faith. Let the truth of the cross be our foundation and the love of God be our lens. Because You gave Yourself for us, we will live fully for You—one step, one day, one act of faith at a time.

In Jesus' name, Amen.

DAY 27

HEARTS SPRINKLED CLEAN

"...having our hearts sprinkled from an evil conscience..."
— Hebrews 10:22 WEB

Lord, I come close—not with fear or shame, but with full assurance because of the blood. You've sprinkled my heart clean. Where guilt once ruled, peace now reigns. My conscience is no longer plagued by sin; it is purified by the sacrifice of Christ.

Let this cleansing go deep. Heal the inner places where memories torment and regrets linger. Let the blood speak louder than accusation. I declare peace of mind and clarity of heart over myself and my household. We will not be ruled by an evil conscience, but by the righteousness You've secured.

Thank You for giving us access to Your presence. We come boldly, not as strangers but as children washed and welcomed. Let the peace of a clean conscience anchor our days and stabilize our souls.

In Jesus' name, Amen.

DAY 28

CRUCIFIED WITH CHRIST

"…our old man was crucified with him…"
— Romans 6:6 WEB

Jesus, I declare today that the old me has died with You. The part of me ruled by sin, fear, and shame was nailed to the cross with Christ. It no longer controls me. Through Your death and resurrection, I am free from the power of sin.

Let this truth become my reality. Remind me daily that I am not a slave to old habits or defeated by temptation. The cross broke sin's grip, and I walk in resurrection life. Let this freedom flow into my home—breaking cycles, healing wounds, and releasing liberty.

Over my family, I declare: the old has passed away. We are new creations. What bound us before no longer defines us. We've been crucified with Christ, and now we live by His power and for His glory.

In Jesus' name, Amen.

DAY 29

LIFE THROUGH COMMUNION

"Whoever eats my flesh and drinks my blood has eternal life…"
— John 6:54 WEB

Jesus, I thank You for the mystery and power of communion with You. You are the Bread of Life, and Your blood is my eternal covenant. When I partake of You—through faith, worship, and daily surrender—I receive life, real life, everlasting life.

Let this truth transform how I approach Your table. It's not a ritual—it's relationship. You offered Your body and poured out Your blood so that I could have unbroken communion with You. Fill my spirit with hunger for more of You. Satisfy my soul with Your presence.

Let my family live in constant connection with the Living Christ. We receive Your life flowing through us—strength for our bodies, joy for our spirits, and grace for every step. Eternal life is not far away—it begins now through fellowship with You.

In Jesus' name, Amen.

DAY 30

CLEANSED BY LIVING WATER

"I will sprinkle clean water on you…"
— Ezekiel 36:25 WEB

Holy God, I praise You for Your promise to cleanse me. You said You would sprinkle clean water on me and wash away all my filth and idols. You are not content with surface change—you desire deep transformation. Thank You for cleansing me by Your Spirit and the blood of Jesus.

Let that water flow freely over my heart. Wash away every compromise, every secret sin, every residue of rebellion. Let Your cleansing not only remove what is wrong but also make room for what is holy. Over my household, I release the purifying presence of the Lord.

We are not defiled—we are clean. We are not distant—we are restored. Let our thoughts, our words, and our actions reflect hearts made pure by God. Clean hands and pure hearts shall be our legacy, by the power of Your Word and Spirit.

In Jesus' name, Amen.

DAY 31

BOUGHT AND PAID FOR BY HIS BLOOD

"...church of God, which he purchased with his own
blood."
— Acts 20:28 WEB

Lord Jesus, I thank You for the ultimate price You paid for me. Your blood was not spilled by accident—it was poured out with purpose. You didn't just redeem a people; You bought us individually, personally, and completely. I am not my own. I am blood-bought and heaven-owned.

Let this truth calm every anxious place in me. I don't belong to fear, guilt, or confusion. I belong to You. You purchased me with blood that cannot be refunded or revoked. Let that reality secure my identity and settle my heart. I was worth dying for—and now I live to glorify the One who gave everything for me.

May my family also rest in this blood-bought peace. We are not abandoned or forgotten. We are the church You died to purchase. Let the weight of our value in Your eyes silence every lie of the enemy. We are precious, chosen, and fully paid for.

In Jesus' name, Amen.

DAY 32

GRATITUDE FOR CHRIST'S MERCY SEAT WORK

> Therefore he was obligated in all things to be made like his brothers, that he might become a merciful and faithful high priest in things pertaining to God, to make atonement for the sins of the people.
> —Hebrews 2:17 WEB

Jesus, my High Priest and Sacrifice, I honor You for becoming the mercy seat on my behalf. You didn't just cover sin—you satisfied justice. You bore the wrath I deserved and turned it into favor. Your blood has forever changed my standing with God.

Thank You for stepping into my place. You didn't plead for mercy from a distance; You became the very offering mercy required. Let gratitude flood my soul for the compassion You showed when You stood in my place. The cross became my mercy seat, and Your blood became my covering.

Let this revelation bring peace into my emotional storms. I am no longer judged, I am justified. I am no longer condemned, I am counted righteous. And my family is under that same mercy. Let us walk humbly, worship deeply, and rejoice fully in Your propitiating love.

In Jesus' name, Amen.

DAY 33

DEEP CLEANSING AND RESTORATION

"Purge me with hyssop, and I will be clean…"
— Psalm 51:7 WEB

Father, I echo David's cry—purge me. Wash me deeply, not just on the surface. Use the hyssop of Your mercy and the power of the blood to reach into the places I've tried to hide. I long not just for forgiveness but for wholeness. Make me truly clean.

Sometimes the stains feel stubborn, the regrets replay too often—but Your cleansing is stronger. What the blood touches, it transforms. Let the cleansing of Jesus reach my thoughts, emotions, and memories. Let shame be uprooted, and let joy be restored. I don't want to be partially healed—I want to be made whole.

Over my family, I declare a fresh washing. Cleanse us from every sin, every habit, every lie we've believed. Let the hyssop of Your Spirit reach our deepest places. You promise we shall be whiter than snow—so let it be. Let peace come through restoration.

In Jesus' name, Amen.

DAY 34

REJOICING IN ERASED RECORDS

"I have blotted out… your sins."
— Isaiah 44:22 WEB

Lord, I rejoice today because the record of my sins is gone. Not covered, not overlooked—blotted out. Like ink washed from a page, the evidence of my failure has vanished beneath the blood of Jesus. There is no longer a case against me in heaven's courtroom.

Let my soul rest in this assurance. I don't have to relive what You've erased. I don't have to rehearse what You've forgotten. You have blotted out my sins like a mist blown away by the morning wind. Teach me to rejoice not in perfection, but in redemption.

For my family, I declare the same joy. No matter how deep the sin or long the history, You've blotted it out. We will not walk around with the weight of old guilt. We will dance in the freedom of clean records and open arms. Let this joy be our strength.

In Jesus' name, Amen.

DAY 35

Walking in the Power of the Covenant

"...This cup is the new covenant in my blood..."
— Luke 22:20 WEB

Jesus, thank You for inviting me into a better covenant—a new and living way sealed with Your blood. When You lifted the cup at the Last Supper, You weren't offering religion, You were offering relationship. You established an unbreakable bond between heaven and earth, sealed not with ink but with blood.

Help me walk in the power of this covenant daily. Let it affect how I pray, how I think, and how I see myself. I am not just saved—I am in covenant with the King. You are committed to me, and I am committed to You. Let covenant peace reign in my heart.

Over my home, I speak covenant security. We are not orphans; we are blood-bound to God. This covenant provides peace, provision, and protection. We claim all that Jesus paid for—because this blood speaks better things.

In Jesus' name, Amen.

DAY 36

Embracing the Blood Fountain

"…a fountain opened… for sin and for uncleanness."
— Zechariah 13:1 WEB

Lord, I thank You for the fountain that flows from Calvary. It is always open, always enough, and always cleansing. This fountain wasn't opened once and then closed—it continues to wash all who come. No sin is too deep, no stain too dark for the flow of Your blood.

Let me run to that fountain every day. Let me not try to clean myself before coming—because it is the fountain that makes me clean. I embrace its power to purify my mind, heal my emotions, and calm my inner storms. This blood is my peace.

I bring my family to the fountain. Let Your cleansing stream flow over our relationships, our words, our choices. Let what was unclean become holy. Let the power of that blood wash over every generation. We stand beneath the fountain—and we are whole.

In Jesus' name, Amen.

DAY 37

THANKSGIVING FOR BLESSED PARDON

"Blessed are those whose iniquities are forgiven…"
— Romans 4:7 WEB

Father, how blessed I am to be forgiven. You didn't just overlook my iniquity—you removed it. You called me blessed not because I've done everything right, but because You made everything right through the blood of Jesus. My sins were many, but Your mercy was more.

Thank You for this incredible pardon. Let gratitude never grow cold in me. Every day I live, every prayer I pray, every blessing I enjoy— it's all because of forgiveness. Let me walk humbly in the awareness of what I've been set free from.

Over my family, I release this same blessedness. We are not cursed—we are forgiven. The enemy has no legal ground because the blood has settled the debt. Let joy replace regret and celebration replace shame. We are the forgiven—and we are free.

In Jesus' name, Amen.

DAY 38

RECEIVING GOD'S FULL FORGIVENESS

"I will remember their sins no more."
— Hebrews 8:12 WEB

Gracious God, Your memory is perfect—yet You choose to forget. You don't just forgive my sins, You refuse to remember them. You don't hold them over my head or revisit them later. Your forgiveness is full, final, and freeing.

Let this truth break every chain of regret. If You don't remember it, I won't relive it. I release every self-accusing thought. I walk away from the prison of my past and into the peace of divine forgetfulness. Your blood has erased the record, and my heart is free.

For my family, I declare this same release. Let no member of our household carry guilt You've already removed. Let the power of forgiveness flow like a river—washing over every relationship, healing every wound, and silencing every accuser.

In Jesus' name, Amen.

DAY 39

JOY IN DIVINE FORGIVENESS

"Blessed is he whose disobedience is forgiven…"
— Psalm 32:1 WEB

Lord, I rejoice in Your forgiveness! You didn't wait for me to fix myself—you stepped in while I was still in disobedience and offered grace. And now, I am blessed—truly, deeply, irreversibly blessed—because You've forgiven me.

Let this joy be more than a moment. Let it fill my days and fuel my worship. I am not under wrath—I am under blessing. Not because I earned it, but because Jesus paid for it with His own blood. Let the freedom of that truth bring laughter to my heart and peace to my soul.

Over my household, I declare joy. Where shame once sat, let singing arise. Where regret lingered, let rejoicing break forth. We are a forgiven family—blessed not by what we've done, but by what Christ has done for us.

In Jesus' name, Amen.

DAY 40

FREEDOM FROM LEGAL ACCUSATIONS

"...blotting out the handwriting... against us..."
— Colossians 2:14 WEB

Jesus, thank You for canceling every legal accusation against me. Every charge the enemy wrote down—every sinful word, thought, and deed—was nailed to Your cross and blotted out by Your blood. The case is closed, and the record is gone.

I refuse to live under the voice of accusation any longer. The handwriting was real, but so was the cross. And Your blood was enough. Let peace fill my mind where torment once ruled. Let me walk freely, fully assured that no charge can stick when You've wiped the record clean.

Over my family, I break every lingering guilt, every legal hold of darkness. The handwriting has been erased. The enemy has lost his case. We walk in freedom, in peace, and in the finished work of the cross.

In Jesus' name, Amen.

DAY 41

DECLARING JESUS AS SAVIOR

"She shall give birth to a son. You shall name him Jesus,
for it is he who shall save his people from their sins."
— Matthew 1:21 WEB

Righteous Redeemer, I boldly declare that Jesus is my Savior, the One appointed by heaven to rescue me from sin's grip. No other name carries the power to cleanse, transform, and deliver. I embrace the full authority of Your saving work. Sin no longer defines me—salvation through Your blood now shapes my destiny.

Let this salvation speak over my household. Every bondage is broken, every stain removed, every chain shattered. We are not a people of guilt—we are a people of grace. Because Jesus saves, no sin is too deep, no pattern too long-standing. We are rescued, redeemed, and released by Your mercy.

Today, I walk in the identity of the saved. I declare peace over my past, freedom in my present, and hope for my future. And my family shall walk in the same. The blood of Jesus is our legacy, our banner, and our shield. We live because the Savior has come—and His name is Jesus.

In Jesus' name, Amen.

DAY 42

CHRIST OUR RANSOM

"Then he is gracious to him, and says, 'Deliver him from going down to the pit. I have found a ransom.'"
— Job 33:24 WEB

Holy Deliverer, I praise You for the ransom that was found—Jesus Christ, the Lamb who took my place. I was destined for the pit, condemned by guilt, and unworthy of redemption, but You spoke mercy and provided blood. The cross became my rescue, and the grave lost its grip.

You didn't delay or debate my worth; You declared it by offering Christ. My soul rejoices in this divine exchange. The sentence over me and my family has been revoked. The curse has no claim, and death has no power. The ransom has been paid—and paid in full by the precious blood of Jesus.

I stand today not as one condemned, but as one delivered. I lift my voice in freedom and call my family into the same liberty. We will not return to the pit; we belong to the redeemed. The ransom speaks louder than accusation. The ransom speaks peace.

In Jesus' name, Amen.

DAY 43

GOD'S MERCY NOT BASED ON MERIT

"I, even I, am he who blots out your transgressions for my
own sake; and I will not remember your sins."
— Isaiah 43:25 WEB

Compassionate Father, I worship You for the mystery of Your
mercy. You chose to blot out my sins not because I earned it, but
because You desired it. Your mercy flows from Your heart—not
from my merit. You remember my failures no more, and that brings
rest to my soul.

You delight in pardoning Your children. You silence the voice of the
accuser with Your own declaration: forgiven. I do not strive for
acceptance—I stand in it. Because of Your covenant, my family and
I are shielded from judgment. We are covered by the blood that
speaks peace and pardon.

Today, I lean into this mercy. I do not try to repay it, only to receive
it. I declare over my life and my family that we are no longer defined
by transgressions but by grace. Your mercy rewrites our story. We
walk boldly, because the blood has made a way.

In Jesus' name, Amen.

DAY 44

RETURNING TO THE FATHER THROUGH GRACE

> "He arose, and came to his father. But while he was still far
> off, his father saw him, and was moved with compassion,
> and ran, and fell on his neck, and kissed him."
> — Luke 15:20 WEB

Abba Father, I arise and return to You today. Even while I was far
off, You saw me. Your eyes never left me, and Your arms never
closed. The kiss of Your acceptance is my peace, and the embrace of
Your grace is my restoration. I come home—not to judgment, but
to joy.

You ran to me with mercy. You clothed me, fed me, and restored
me. And You've done the same for my household. Though we
strayed, Your love never did. Though we wandered, Your covenant
remained. Your blood has made the way back, and we walk it
boldly.

I declare that no shame shall keep us from Your embrace. No failure
shall disqualify us from Your table. We are sons and daughters, not
servants of shame. You've run to us, and now we run in freedom,
wrapped in robes of righteousness.

In Jesus' name, Amen.

DAY 45

Bold Declaration of Forgiveness

"Be it known to you therefore, brothers, that through this
man is proclaimed to you remission of sins."
— Acts 13:38 WEB

Living Word, I proclaim it boldly and without apology—through
Jesus Christ, my sins are forgiven. Not delayed, not pending, but
fully remitted. I will not whisper this truth in shame; I will declare
it in victory. The blood of Jesus has finished the work.

Let this truth echo in my home. I declare forgiveness over every
member of my family. We do not carry guilt passed down through
generations. We do not wear labels of failure. We are a forgiven
people, called righteous by the blood of the Lamb. His forgiveness
rewrites our name.

I embrace this proclamation as my daily confession. Sin's power is
broken, its voice silenced, its grip destroyed. The man Christ Jesus
has spoken—and I believe it. Forgiveness reigns in this house.
Mercy lives in our hearts. And peace is our portion.

In Jesus' name, Amen.

DAY 46

WORSHIP FROM A FORGIVEN HEART

"But there is forgiveness with you, therefore you are feared."
— Psalm 130:4 WEB

Awesome and Holy One, I bow before You with a heart drenched in gratitude. You are not a God who delights in wrath, but One who forgives with depth and desire. Your forgiveness awakens reverence in me—deep, trembling worship birthed from mercy received.

I do not fear You because of punishment—I revere You because of pardon. You forgave me when I couldn't forgive myself. You lifted me from the depths and crowned me with compassion. My soul magnifies You, and my family joins the song. We are not forgotten—we are forgiven.

Let every room in our home be filled with the sound of praise. Let worship rise not from perfection, but from mercy. We bow before You not to earn grace, but to honor it. You are worthy of all our love because You gave all to love us.

In Jesus' name, Amen.

DAY 47

CALLING ON GOD'S FORGIVING NATURE

"To the Lord our God belong mercies and forgiveness; for
we have rebelled against him."
— Daniel 9:9 WEB

Faithful God, I lift my voice to the One in whom mercy dwells.
Forgiveness is not just something You do—it is who You are.
Though I have rebelled, You remain ready. Though we have strayed,
Your nature has not changed. You are the God of pardon.

Today I fall upon Your mercy and call it forth for my life and my
family. Where rebellion once ruled, let reconciliation reign. Let the
power of Your forgiving nature flood our hearts. You are not a
distant judge—you are a covenant Father, rich in compassion.

Let my home be a sanctuary of second chances. Let the legacy of
forgiveness erase the record of rebellion. I trust in who You are
more than in what I've done. You are merciful, and You delight to
forgive.

In Jesus' name, Amen.

DAY 48

Confession That Leads to Mercy

"He who conceals his sins doesn't prosper, but whoever
confesses and forsakes them shall have mercy."
— Proverbs 28:13 WEB

Righteous Judge and Loving Father, I come with open hands and an
unveiled heart. I hide nothing from You. I confess what You already
see—not to inform You, but to invite You. I forsake the paths that
led me away from peace, and I run toward mercy.

Your Word is clear—confession is the key to mercy. So I release
every hidden weight, every secret sin, every buried wound. I trade
secrecy for restoration. Let mercy rise like the morning over me and
my family. Let honesty break the power of darkness and usher in
divine healing.

I declare this over my household: We are not a people of cover-up—
we are a people of clean hands and pure hearts. Where sin once
lingered, grace now rules. Because we confess and forsake, we walk
in mercy that never ends.

In Jesus' name, Amen.

DAY 49

ATONEMENT FULFILLED IN CHRIST

"For on this day shall atonement be made for you, to cleanse you. You shall be clean from all your sins before Yahweh."
— Leviticus 16:30 WEB

High Priest of Heaven, I honor You for the once-for-all atonement You made by Your own blood. The day of atonement is no longer a yearly hope—it is a finished reality. I stand clean, not by ritual, but by redemption. The veil was torn, and the way was opened.

Let this cleansing touch every part of my being. Body, soul, and spirit—washed in the blood. Let my family stand in this same confidence. We do not await atonement—we live in it. Our sins are not postponed—they are purged. The work is complete.

I declare that no accusation can stand. No guilt can survive. The blood has spoken, and it speaks "clean." We live under the banner of atonement. And because of Jesus, we walk in peace with God forever.

In Jesus' name, Amen.

DAY 50

SALVATION THROUGH CONFESSION AND BELIEF

> "That if you will confess with your mouth that Jesus is Lord, and believe in your heart that God raised him from the dead, you will be saved."
> — Romans 10:9 WEB

King Jesus, I confess boldly and believe deeply—You are Lord, risen and reigning. Your blood has purchased my salvation, and I declare it with joy. I am not hoping for salvation—I have received it. I am saved by grace through faith, and I will not be silent about it.

Let this confession echo through my home. Let every heart in my family confess Jesus as Lord and believe unto salvation. We are not lost—we are found. We are not bound—we are free. The blood has opened the door, and faith has brought us in.

I speak salvation into every corner of my life. My mouth will declare it, my heart will believe it, and my home will reflect it. Jesus is Lord—and because of that, we are saved.

In Jesus' name, Amen.

DAY 51

Living In Covenantal Pardon

"Moses took the blood and sprinkled it on the people, and said, 'Look, this is the blood of the covenant, which Yahweh has made with you concerning all these words.'"
— Exodus 24:8 WEB

O Lord, Covenant-Keeping God, I thank You for the blood of Jesus, the Mediator of the new and better covenant. This blood was not sprinkled from bulls or goats, but from Your spotless Son—shed once and for all for the redemption of my soul. I step into the covering of that covenant today. Let the power of that blood speak on behalf of my family and me, marking us as Your own and securing our eternal pardon.

Father, I receive the benefits of this unbreakable bond—mercy instead of wrath, forgiveness instead of judgment, peace instead of fear. Your covenant stands stronger than every accusation of the enemy. Even when I fall short, Your blood reaffirms Your love and commitment to restore me. May this covenant not only cleanse but consecrate my household to You.

Seal us, Lord, by the covenantal power of the blood. Let no curse, no guilt, and no shame override what Jesus finished on the cross. Let this blood speak louder than our past and louder than the voice of condemnation. In the name of Jesus, we are forgiven, accepted, and forever Yours.

In Jesus' name, Amen.

DAY 52

APPEAL TO GOD'S MERCY

"Have mercy on me, God, according to your loving
kindness. According to the multitude of your tender
mercies, blot out my transgressions."
— Psalm 51:1 WEB

Merciful Father, I cry out to You from the depths of a heart humbled
by grace. You are the God of lovingkindness and compassion, and
I run to You, not away from You. I do not come on the basis of my
merit but on the basis of the blood—perfect, precious, and
powerful—shed by Your Son.

Let the flood of mercy that flowed from Calvary wash over me and
my family. Let every transgression be blotted out by Your divine
eraser. Where the enemy tries to etch guilt into our minds, I appeal
to Your lovingkindness to blot it out. Your mercy doesn't just
overlook—it erases and restores. You are not reluctant to forgive
but eager to restore.

Today I lift my family before You, covered in the blood, and cry for
mercy over every area of sin, failure, or shame. Let the stronghold
of condemnation be shattered, and let the grace of Your presence
come rushing in like a river. May we live in the joy of those who are
forgiven.

In Jesus' name, Amen.

DAY 53

HEART-LEVEL REPENTANCE

"Tear your heart, and not your garments, and turn to
Yahweh, your God; for he is gracious and merciful..."
— Joel 2:13 WEB

Gracious Redeemer, I don't just offer words—I bring my broken
heart. I rend it open before You, God, not with outward display, but
inward surrender. I return not with pretense but with passion,
because I know You are gracious, slow to anger, and abounding in
mercy.

Lord, let my repentance go beyond the surface. Let it be the cry of
my soul and the posture of my life. I refuse to live a double life—
draw me into true surrender by the power of Your blood. As I turn,
turn my entire family toward You. Let generational guilt be lifted as
we fall into Your grace.

Blood of Jesus, speak over every wound, every compromise, and
every delay. Cleanse us thoroughly and lead us into new life. May
our hearts burn once again for what burns in Yours. We return
because You welcome us—not with wrath, but with outstretched
arms.

In Jesus' name, Amen.

DAY 54

JESUS, OUR INTERCESSOR WHEN WE FALL

"My little children, I write these things to you so that you
may not sin. If anyone sins, we have a Counselor with the
Father, Jesus Christ, the righteous."
— 1 John 2:1 WEB

Heavenly Advocate, I thank You that even when I fall, I am not
forsaken. You, Jesus, stand at the right hand of the Father,
interceding on my behalf. When the accuser raises his voice, Your
blood silences him. When guilt rises, Your advocacy rises higher
still.

Thank You, Lord, that my sins don't surprise You, and they don't
separate me when I run to You. You stand in the courtroom of
heaven, not pleading for leniency but presenting the final verdict—
paid in full. For every stumble, You offer strength. For every fall,
You offer forgiveness.

Let this same intercession extend over my household. For every
family member trapped in shame or struggling in silence, let Your
advocacy rise. Pull them from the pit. Restore them by grace. May
they know You not as judge but as the Redeemer who never stops
fighting for us.

In Jesus' name, Amen.

DAY 55

Silencing Guilt and Accusation

"I heard a loud voice in heaven, saying... the accuser of
our brothers has been thrown down..."
— Revelation 12:10 WEB

Warrior of Heaven, I lift my voice in triumph today! The blood has
already spoken, and the accuser has already fallen. No longer does
guilt have a grip, and no longer does shame have a seat in my story.
I declare: every accusing voice against my life and family is cast
down by the authority of the blood.

Let the cry of heaven echo in my spirit—"Not guilty!" I refuse to
rehearse what You've already redeemed. I renounce every
whispered lie, every false identity, every guilt-laced memory that
haunts the mind. The blood testifies better things than judgment—
it proclaims freedom.

Lord, let the blood of Jesus silence the voice of every curse, every
generational guilt, and every internal torment. We are not defined
by accusation but by adoption. Today, I walk free—my head lifted,
my spirit clean, my name written in the Lamb's Book of Life.

In Jesus' name, Amen.

DAY 56

COMING BOLDLY FOR MERCY AND GRACE

"Let's therefore draw near with boldness to the throne of
grace, that we may receive mercy…"
— Hebrews 4:16 WEB

King of Grace, I come running—not crawling—into Your presence
today. By the blood of Jesus, the veil has been torn and the throne
has been opened wide. I come boldly because the price has been
fully paid. I bring my weaknesses, my needs, and my family to You.

Let Your throne be a fountain of mercy for us. Let Your grace pour
into every dry place. For every weary soul in my household, I ask
for renewal. For every hidden fear, I ask for peace. For every
lingering sin, I ask for cleansing. You don't turn us away; You invite
us closer.

Father, I declare that we are a family marked by bold access. We are
not orphans—we are blood-washed children. Let the atmosphere
of heaven break into our home. Let mercy reign over
condemnation. Let grace triumph over struggle. Let us live in the
joy of constant communion with You.

In Jesus' name, Amen.

DAY 57

REDEEMED FROM JUDGMENT

"Christ redeemed us from the curse of the law, having become a curse for us..."
— Galatians 3:13 WEB

Redeeming Lamb of God, I stand in awe of the exchange made at Calvary. You didn't just forgive my sins—you became the curse so I could walk in blessing. You absorbed the judgment that was meant for me. I declare: my family and I are no longer under the curse—we are covered by the cross.

Every form of judgment—spiritual, emotional, or physical—was broken the moment Your blood was shed. I cancel every generational curse, every legal claim of the enemy, and every lingering shadow of the past. By the blood, we are redeemed from failure, sickness, poverty, and shame.

Let the blessing flow, not just over me, but over my lineage. I plead the blood over my children, their destiny, and their dreams. Let every curse stop with me. Let a new cycle of grace begin. We walk in the blessing—not by effort but by inheritance.

In Jesus' name, Amen.

DAY 58

Complete Salvation In Christ

"...he is able to save to the uttermost those who draw near
to God through him..."
— Hebrews 7:25 WEB

Great High Priest, I exalt You today for a salvation that knows no limits. You don't just save partially—you save completely. You save my past, redeem my present, and secure my eternal future. You save my whole household to the uttermost.

No situation is too far gone, no soul too stained. By Your eternal priesthood, You stand before the Father with blood that never loses its power. I call upon that saving power for every family member— those near, those far, those wandering, those weary. Let Your blood reach and rescue.

God of total restoration, I declare salvation over our minds, emotions, habits, and relationships. Rescue us to the depths of our being. Make us trophies of grace, shining with the evidence of a salvation that never ends.

In Jesus' name, Amen.

DAY 59

CHRIST CAME TO SAVE, NOT CONDEMN

"For God didn't send his Son into the world to judge the
world, but that the world should be saved through him."
— John 3:17 WEB

Father of Mercy, I thank You for sending Jesus—not to point a
finger but to open Your arms. You did not come to condemn me,
You came to claim me. Your love has rescued me from wrath and
brought me into the safety of salvation.

I reject every voice that says I am unworthy, disqualified, or
forsaken. Jesus, You came to heal what was broken, not to punish.
Let that truth ring in my ears louder than every lie. I receive Your
saving grace with joy and reverence. Let my family know this love
too—fully and forever.

May our home be a dwelling place of mercy, not condemnation. Let
every child, every spouse, every loved one feel the warmth of Your
saving light. We are not condemned—we are celebrated as those
brought near by the blood.

In Jesus' name, Amen.

DAY 60

PRAISE FOR NATIONAL AND PERSONAL PARDON

"You have forgiven the iniquity of your people. You have covered all their sin."
— Psalm 85:2 WEB

Forgiving Father, I lift my hands in gratitude. You have not only forgiven me personally, but You have covered the iniquity of an entire people. I join in that ancient song of deliverance and declare: blessed is the nation, the family, the soul whose sins are covered by the blood.

Lord, let Your mercy flood every area of our land and every heart in our home. From the leaders of our nation to the youngest child in our family, let the power of the blood bring cleansing. Revive us again, O Lord, and let Your forgiveness be the foundation of our future.

Today I praise You not only for what You have done, but for what You are doing—restoring the broken, reviving the weary, and rebuilding what was torn down. We are a forgiven people. We are a redeemed generation. We are a family marked by grace.

In Jesus' name, Amen.

EPILOGUE

You've reached the end of this book—but not the end of your journey in the blood.

Each Scripture you've prayed, every declaration you've made, and every tear that may have fallen in repentance or release has been gathered by the Father. The blood of Jesus has not only cleansed your past—it now testifies of your freedom, your righteousness, and your restored relationship with God.

You are no longer bound to shame. No longer held hostage by condemnation. You have been pardoned by the highest authority in heaven and earth—the Righteous Judge—and no accuser can reverse His verdict. The cross was enough. The blood still speaks. And it speaks *mercy* over you.

But this is just the beginning.

Let what you've experienced in these pages become your new rhythm: walking daily in the awareness of Christ's pardon, extending that same mercy to others, and boldly accessing the presence of God with a clean conscience.

May this book mark a turning point for you—a sacred reset where sin no longer defines you, and grace becomes your anthem.

Go forward, not in guilt—but in glory.

You are blood-washed, blood-sealed, and blood-covered. Live forgiven. Live free.

In Jesus' name, Amen.

ENCOURAGE OTHERS WITH YOUR STORY

If this prayer guide has strengthened your faith, deepened your intercession, or helped you stand in the gap, would you consider leaving a short review on Amazon? Your feedback not only encourages others but also helps more believers discover this resource and join in the prayer movement. Every review—just a few sentences—makes a difference. Thank you for being part of this movement.

PROTECTION THROUGH THE BLOOD:

60 DAYS OF PRAYERS FOR LIVING UNTOUCHABLE UNDER CHRIST'S BLOOD

You are not helpless. You are not exposed. You are covered— completely—by the blood of Jesus.

In a world of rising dangers, demonic assaults, and spiritual unpredictability, Protection Through the Blood equips you and your family to live untouchable under the supernatural shield of Christ's blood. Every day's entry is a power-packed prayer experience rooted in Scripture—designed to build a blood-line barrier around your life, home, and destiny.. Part of *The Blood Covenant Series*, this second volume is a must-have companion for believers who refuse to live defenseless in a dark world. If you're ready to activate heaven's strongest defense system and stand boldly in the shadow of the Almighty, this 60-day journey is for you.

Live bold. Live covered. Live untouchable—through the blood.

PREVAIL THROUGH THE BLOOD:

60 DAYS OF PRAYERS FOR SPIRITUAL MASTERY OVER THE ENEMY

What if every scheme of the enemy against your life could be dismantled—by one unstoppable weapon?

In *Prevail Through the Blood*, you'll discover how to wield the most powerful force in the universe—the Blood of Jesus Christ—to overcome every spiritual assault, shatter generational yokes, and walk in daily victory. This is more than a prayer book. It is your 60-day spiritual war manual, designed to train your hands for battle and your heart for triumph. This third installment in The Blood Covenant Series invites you into a journey of spiritual mastery. Whether you are in the heat of battle or standing in victory, every page will sharpen your discernment, stir your faith, and saturate your home in the protective power of Christ's blood.

Break free from every chain. Pray with fire. Win with the Blood.

PRESERVATION THROUGH THE BLOOD:

60 DAYS OF PRAYERS FOR DIVINE HEALING AND WHOLENESS

Unlock Lasting Healing and Wholeness Through the Blood of Jesus

Preservation Through the Blood: 60 Days of Prayers for Divine Healing and Wholeness is your prophetic, Scripture-packed guide to receiving total restoration in your body, soul, and spirit through the covenant power of Christ's blood. More than a devotional, this book is a healing altar—built on 60 carefully selected Bible verses that directly reveal God's will to heal and preserve you.

Whether you're battling chronic illness, emotional trauma, lingering symptoms, or generational afflictions, these blood-based prayers will speak directly to the root of the issue to appropriate divine healing. This book equips you to confront the source, not just the symptoms.

PROSPERITY THROUGH THE BLOOD:

60 DAYS OF PRAYERS FOR UNLOCKING HEAVEN'S WEALTH AND WALKING IN COVENANT INCREASE

You were redeemed for more than survival—
you were redeemed to prosper.

In a world filled with economic uncertainty, God's promise of abundance still stands. *Prosperity Through the Blood: 60 Days of Prayers for Unlocking Heaven's Wealth and Walking in Covenant Increase* invites you into a powerful journey of discovering what the blood of Jesus truly purchased for you—not just eternal life, but a full, flourishing, and prosperous life on earth. Whether you're in a season of financial need or simply hungry to experience more of what belongs to you in Christ, *Prosperity Through the Blood* is your roadmap to living untouchable, unshakable, and abundantly blessed under the power of the blood.

PEACE THROUGH THE BLOOD:

60 DAYS OF PRAYERS FOR RESTING IN THE COVENANT OF UNSHAKABLE PEACE

Are you ready to silence every storm of the mind, heart, and home—once and for all?

Peace is not the absence of problems—it is the presence of Christ Himself. And through the blood of His cross, that peace has already been purchased, sealed, and placed into your covenant inheritance. You don't have to fight for it—you only have to receive and enforce it.

This book is your daily guide to experiencing heaven's calm in every circumstance. Rooted in Colossians 1:20—"having made peace through the blood of his cross"—this book will lead you into prophetic, Scripture-anchored prayers that confront anxiety, heal emotional wounds, restore fractured relationships, and anchor your soul in God's unshakable rest.

COMMAND YOUR MORNING: 30 DAYS OF PRAYERS AND DECLARATIONS TO SEIZE YOUR DAY AND SHAPE YOUR DESTINY

There is a battle over every morning—and every believer must choose to either drift into the day or command it.

Command Your Morning: 30 Days of Prayers and Declarations to Seize Your Day and Shape Your Destiny is a spiritually charged guide to help you start each day with purpose, power, and prophetic clarity. This is more than a devotional—it's a call to action. Each day in this 30-day journey is built around **five core biblical themes** that set the spiritual tone for your day: **Praise, Purpose, Protection, Provision** and **Position**. Don't just wake up. Command your morning—and shape your destiny.

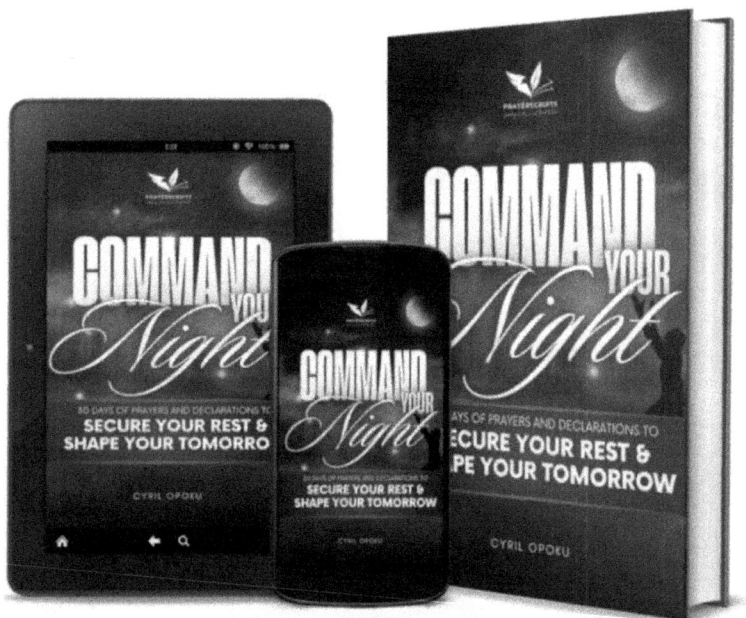

COMMAND YOUR NIGHT: 30 DAYS OF PRAYERS AND DECLARATIONS TO SECURE YOUR REST AND SHAPE YOUR TOMORROW

Every night is a spiritual battlefield—what you do before you sleep can determine the course of your tomorrow.

Command Your Night: 30 Days of Prayers and Declarations to Secure Your Rest and Shape Your Tomorrow is a powerful devotional prayer manual designed to help you end each day in victory, not vulnerability. Whether you're battling anxiety, spiritual attacks, restlessness, or simply longing for deeper peace, this book equips you to reclaim your night with bold, Scripture-rooted prayers. Each night is structured around five strategic prayer themes: *Shut, Shield, Silence, Show, Sleep.*

COMMAND YOUR EVENING: 30 DAYS OF PRAYERS AND DECLARATIONS TO RELEASE THE DAY AND RECLAIM INTIMACY WITH GOD

There is a battle over every transition—and evening is one of the most spiritually neglected.

Command Your Evening is the third book in the **Command Your Destiny** series—following *Command Your Morning* and *Command Your Night*. In heaven's rhythm, the evening is not just a wind-down—it's a window. A sacred hour where destinies are recalibrated, burdens are lifted, and hearts are re-centered in the presence of God. In *Command Your Evening*, you'll journey through 30 days of intentional, Spirit-led prayers and prophetic declarations centered around five key evening themes: **Release, Renew, Refocus, Rebuild,** and **Rest**.

SCRIPTURES & PRAYERS FOR DELIVERANCE FROM TROUBLE:

40 DAYS OF PRAYER FOR WHEN LIFE FEELS OVERWHELMING

Are you walking through a season where life feels heavy, hope feels distant, and your prayers feel weak?

Scriptures & Prayers for Deliverance from Trouble is a 40-day journey of honest prayers and powerful Scriptures to help you find peace, strength, and healing when life is overwhelming. Each day offers a personal, Scripture-based prayer written in the language of real faith and raw trust. This devotional isn't about perfect words—it's about real connection with God when you need Him most.

SCRIPTURES & PRAYERS FOR DELIVERANCE FROM EVIL:

50 DAYS OF PRAYER TO OVERCOME DARKNESS AND FIND GOD'S
PROTECTION

When darkness presses in, how do you pray?

When fear grips your heart or unseen battles rage around you, you
need more than generic words—you need Scripture, truth, and the
steady hand of God to lead you through.

*Scriptures & Prayers for Deliverance from Evil: 50 Days of Prayer to
Overcome Darkness and Find God's Protection* is a powerful
devotional journey designed to help you pray boldly and biblically
through seasons of spiritual warfare, oppression, fear, or
uncertainty.

SCRIPTURES & PRAYERS FOR ENGAGING THE ENEMY:

70 DAYS OF PRAYER TO REBUKE THE ENEMY AND RELEASE GOD'S POWER

You weren't called to run from the battle—

you were anointed to win it.

Scriptures & Prayers for Engaging the Enemy: 70 Days of Prayer to Rebuke the Enemy and Release God's Power is a bold devotional for believers who are ready to rise, resist, and reclaim what the enemy has tried to steal. If you're tired of feeling spiritually outnumbered, this book will equip you to fight back—with Scripture in your mouth and power in your prayers. Over 70 days, you'll be guided through five strategic phases of spiritual warfare: (1) Rebuking the Enemy, (2) Releasing Terror Upon the Enemy (3) Praying for the Fall of the Enemy (4) Treading Upon the Enemy (5) When Heaven Strikes.

The war is real. But so is your victory.

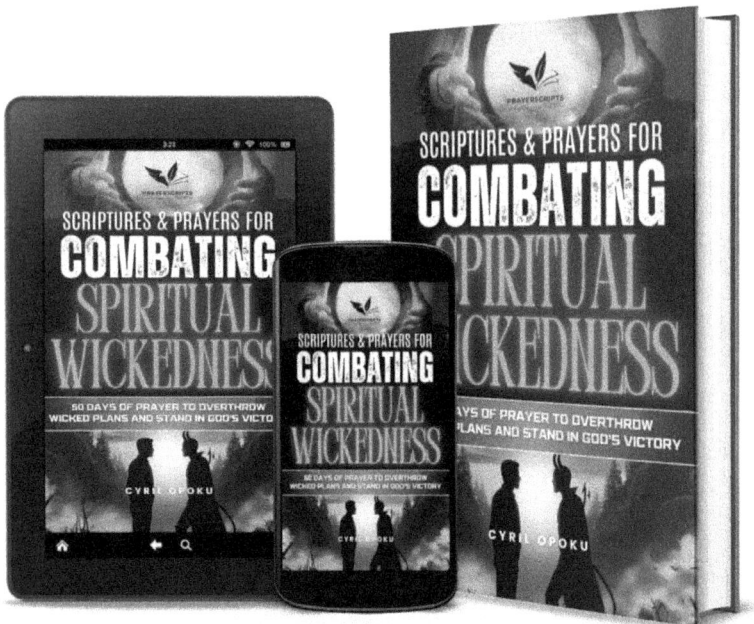

SCRIPTURES & PRAYERS FOR COMBATING SPIRITUAL WICKEDNESS:

50 DAYS OF PRAYER TO OVERTHROW WICKED PLANS AND STAND IN GOD'S VICTORY

Are you facing opposition that feels deeper than the natural? Do you sense hidden resistance working against your progress, peace, or purpose? You're not imagining it—and you're not powerless.

Rooted in the authority of Scripture and fueled by bold, targeted prayers, *Scriptures & Prayers for Combating Spiritual Wickedness* equips you to confront darkness head-on. Each day features a focused Bible passage and a heartfelt, Scripture-based prayer designed to nullify ungodly counsel, disrupt demonic schemes, and establish God's victory in every area of your life.

STANDING IN THE GAP FOR COVENANT AWAKENING:

30 DAYS OF PRAYER FOR NATIONAL REPENTANCE, RIGHTEOUS LEADERSHIP & GOD'S SOVEREIGN RULE

What if your prayers could help turn the tide of a nation?

America stands at a spiritual crossroads. Division deepens, truth is under siege, and righteousness is being redefined. But God is still searching for those who will stand in the gap—intercessors who will cry out for mercy, justice, and national awakening.

Standing in the Gap for Covenant Awakening is a 30-day prayer guide for believers who sense the urgency of the hour and long to see their nation return to God.

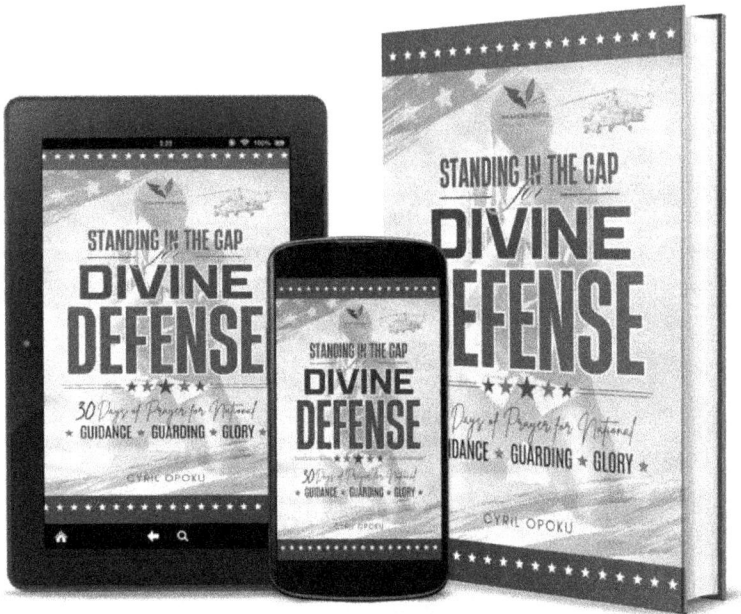

STANDING IN THE GAP FOR DIVINE DEFENSE:

30 DAYS OF PRAYER FOR NATIONAL GUIDANCE, GUARDING & GLORY

When the foundations of a nation feel as if they're shaking, prayer is the strongest fortress you can build.

Standing in the Gap for Divine Defense: 30 Days of Prayer for National Guidance, Guarding & Glory is your call to action—a 30-day journey of powerful, Scripture-rooted intercession that invites everyday believers to become watchmen on the walls for their nation. Drawing on timeless truths from God's Word, this devotional equips you to stand in the gap for your nation and **Seek Heaven's Wisdom, Secure Divine Protection,** and **Ignite Spiritual Awakening.** If you sense the urgency of the hour and long to see your country guided and guarded by the hand of God, open these pages. Stand in the gap. Watch Him move.

STANDING IN THE GAP FOR NATIONAL HEALING:

<u>40 DAYS OF PRAYER FOR RECONCILIATION, RIGHTEOUSNESS, AND RESTORATION</u>

What if your prayers could help heal a nation? What if God is waiting for someone—like you—to stand in the gap?

Standing in the Gap for National Healing: 40 Days of Prayer for Reconciliation, Righteousness, and Restoration is a bold, Spirit-filled call to action for believers who refuse to sit on the sidelines while their nation drifts further from God. In a time marked by division, confusion, and moral decline, this book equips you to pray with power, precision, and unshakable hope. Inside, you'll find 40 days of Scripture-based intercession divided into three strategic sections: **Peace, Unity & Reconciliation, Morality, Truth & Righteous Leadership,** and **National Restoration & Reformation.** It's time to stop watching history unfold—and start shaping it in prayer.

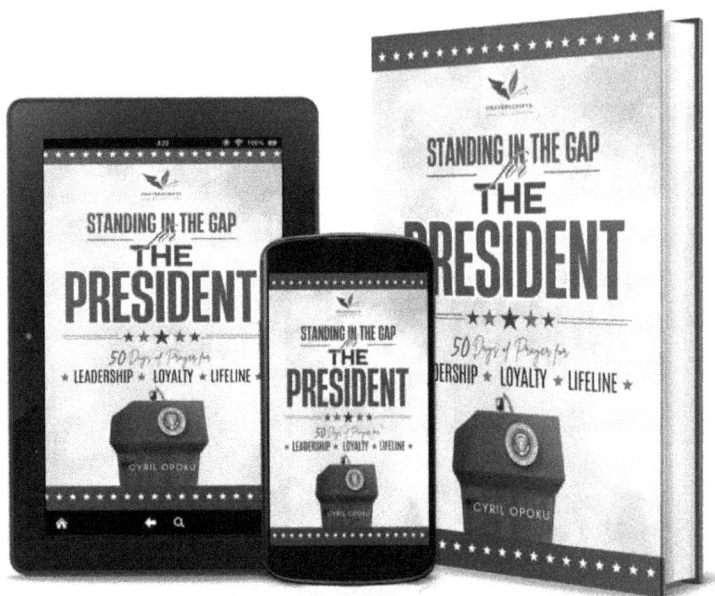

STANDING IN THE GAP FOR THE PRESIDENT:

50 DAYS OF PRAYER FOR LEADERSHIP, LOYALTY, AND LIFELINE

When a nation's leader is under spiritual siege, will you answer the call to stand in the gap?

Standing in the Gap for The President: 50 Days of Prayer for Leadership, Loyalty, and Lifeline is a bold, Scripture-saturated prayer guide for those who understand that the battles facing our leaders are more than political—they are spiritual. Assassination attempts, betrayal from within, and attacks on character and conscience are not just headlines—they're signs of the times. Inside, you'll find 50 days of strategic intercession divided into three high-impact sections: **Presidential Character & Leadership**, **Against Disloyal Insiders**, and **Against Assassination Attempts**. The future of a nation can shift through the prayers of the faithful. It's time to stand in the gap.

www.ingramcontent.com/pod-product-compliance
Lightning Source LLC
Chambersburg PA
CBHW062020040426
42447CB00010B/2081